nicholas of myra

Giver of Many Gifts

270–345/352
Born in present-day Turkey
Feast Day: December 6
Patronage:
Children, Russia, brides, sailors

Text by Barbara Yoffie
Illustrated by Katherine A. Borgatti

Liguori

Dedication

To my family:
my parents Jim and Peg,
my husband Bill,
our son Sam and daughter-in-law Erin,
and our precious grandchildren
Ben, Lucas, and Andrew

To all the children I have had the privilege of teaching throughout the years.

Imprimi Potest:
Harry Grile, CSsR, Provincial
Denver Province, The Redemptorists

Published by Liguori Publications
Liguori, Missouri 63057

To order, call 800-325-9521
www.liguori.org

p ISBN: 978-0-7648-2331-2
e ISBN: 978-0-7648-6848-1

Liguori Publications, a nonprofit corporation, is an apostolate of The Redemptorists. To learn more about The Redemptorists, visit Redemptorists.com.

Printed in the United States of America
17 16 15 14 13 / 5 4 3 2 1
First Edition

Dear Parents and Teachers:

Saints and Me! is a series of children's books about saints, with six books in each set. The first set is titled *Saints of North America*. This second set, *Saints of Christmas,* selects seven heavenly heroes who teach us to love the Infant Jesus. Some saints in this set have feast days within Advent and Christmas time, but others are celebrated within ordinary time and Easter time. We selected these saints based on their connection to the Christmas story and how they inspire us to let the mystery of Christ's birth grow within our hearts.

Saints of Christmas includes the heroic lives of seven saints from different times and places who loved Jesus. Saints Mary and Joseph witnessed the miracle of God's abundant love for humanity as our Infant Savior entered the world to bring us home to God. Saint Lucy followed Jesus in a time when Christianity was against the law. The story of Saint Nicholas was so incredible that it inspired our secular notion of Santa Claus. Saint Francis of Assisi added much flavor to our current Christmas traditions. Saint Martin de Porres was a biracial saint who taught us about divine love for all people. And a saint of our own era, Gianna Beretta Molla, witnessed a deep belief in the gift of life.

Which saint cared for slaves from Africa? Who became a doctor and mother? What saints were present at Jesus' birth in Bethlehem? Who desired to be a knight? Which saint was a bishop of a seaport city? Do you know which saint's name means "light?" Find the answers in the *Saints of Christmas* set, part of the *Saints and Me!* series, and help your child identify with the lives of the saints.

Introduce your children or students to the *Saints and Me!* series as they:

—**READ** about the lives of the saints and are inspired by their stories.

—**PRAY** to the saints for their intercession.

—**CELEBRATE** the saints and relate to their lives.

saints of christmas

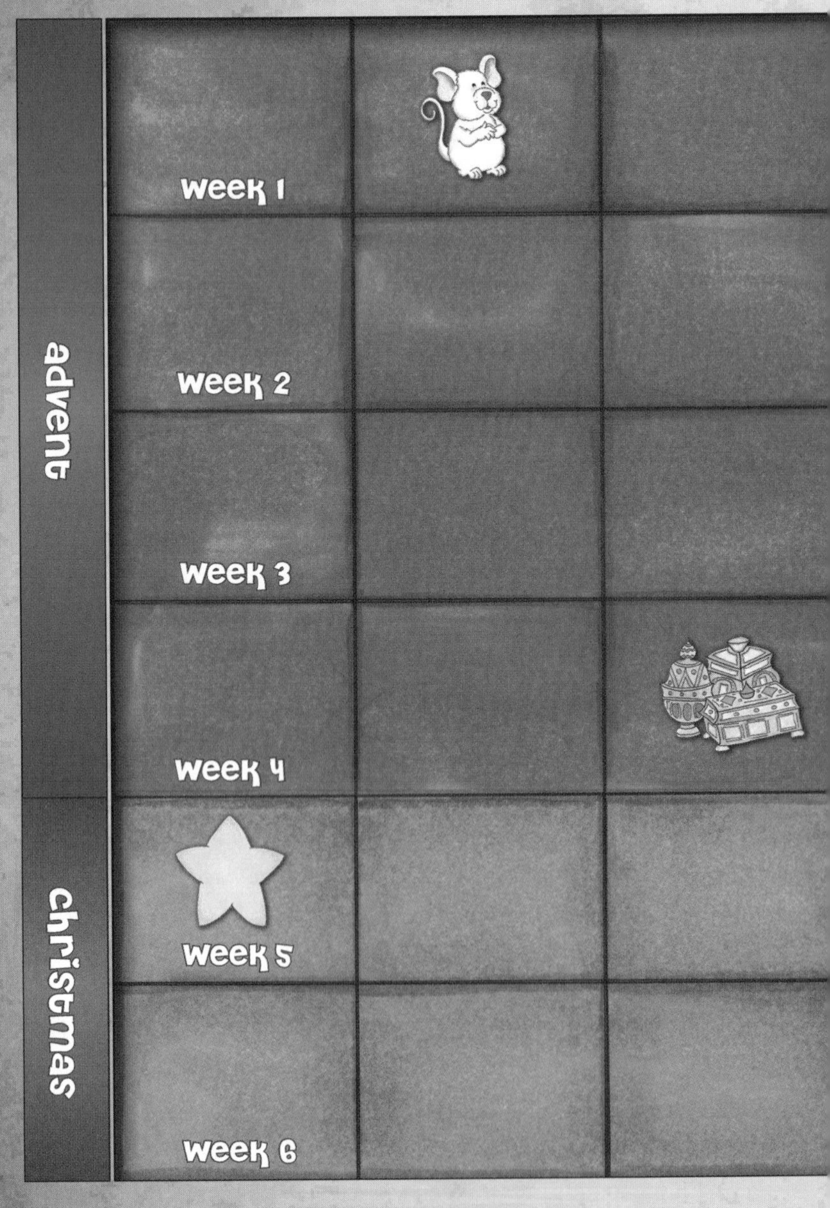

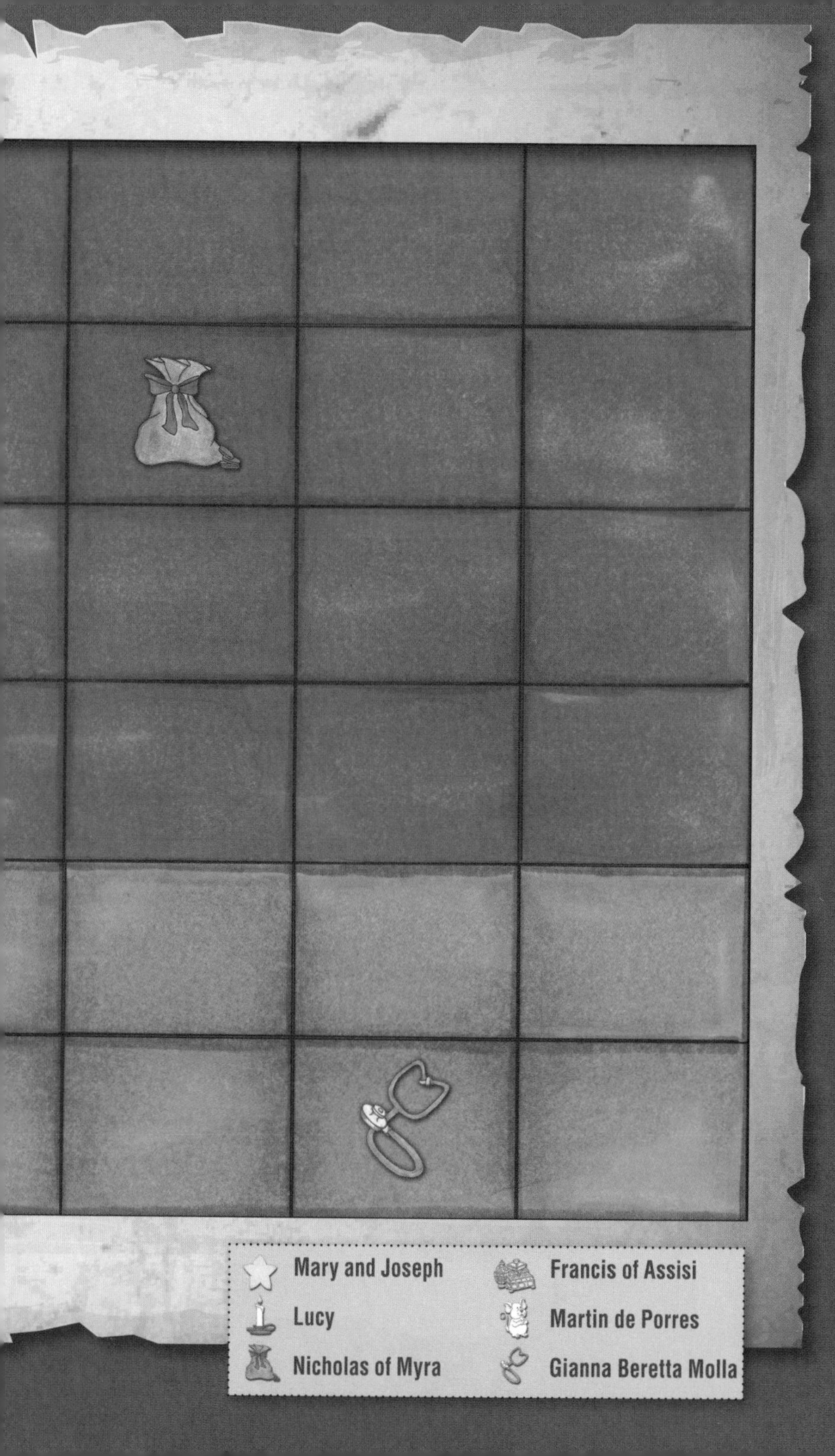

Mary and Joseph
Francis of Assisi
Lucy
Martin de Porres
Nicholas of Myra
Gianna Beretta Molla

Saint Nicholas lived a long, long time ago. There are many wonderful stories told about Saint Nicholas. He is a popular saint in the Church and is celebrated in countries around the world.

Nicholas was born in the town of Patara in the country now called Turkey. His parents taught him about God. They taught him how to pray. They also taught Nicholas how to share with others.

People liked Nicholas because he was friendly and kind. He was always ready to help. And he didn't want anything in return, not even a thank you.

One day he heard about a man in town who needed help. He had three daughters. The girls needed money so they could get married. In those days, a woman's family gave money or property to the family of the man she was going to marry.

But the man in town was so poor he had no property. He had only a few coins. "What shall I do? My daughters will never be married," he cried to himself. He was very sad.

Nicholas had an idea. That night he went to the poor man's house. He threw a small bag of gold through an open window. The next day the man found the gold. Now one daughter could get married!

Nicholas went to the house two more nights with small bags of gold. On the third night, the man saw Nicholas and thanked him, saying, "You are so kind. All of my daughters can get married now!"

Years later, Nicholas became the bishop of Myra, a city by the sea. As bishop he taught the people about God. He defended the faith and helped the poor. Bishop Nicholas treated people fairly.

Three prisoners were in trouble. They were going to be put to death. But they were not guilty. So Bishop Nicholas went to talk to the governor. “These men are innocent!” he shouted. The governor changed his mind and let the prisoners go free.

The people of Myra had a big problem. They went to see Bishop Nicholas. "There is no food, and our children are hungry," they said. Bishop Nicholas knew there were ships in the harbor. And he knew the ships were filled with grain.

He went to see the captain of a big ship. “Please share your grain with my people. We are very hungry,” he begged. “This grain is for another city,” the captain said. Bishop Nicholas asked the captain again. “I promise you, the grain will not be missed,” he said with a smile.

The captain decided to give the holy bishop some bags of grain. Bishop Nicholas thanked the captain and took the grain to the hungry people. When the ship arrived at the next port there was plenty of grain left. Bishop Nicholas was right! No one noticed the missing bags.

After his death, people told exciting stories about Bishop Nicholas all the time. They remembered his holy life and kind actions. He was loved by all. Many people started calling him Saint Nicholas.

Sailors told famous stories about him in every port. They believed he helped them when they were in trouble at sea. Sometimes sailors would pray to Saint Nicholas.

When there was a big storm at sea they prayed, “Help us, Saint Nicholas!” If they were lost or afraid they prayed again. “Good Saint Nicholas, keep us safe.”

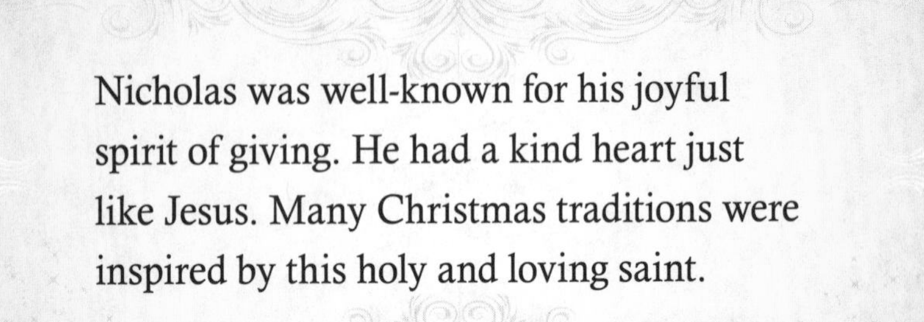

Be kind and be fair.
Show all people you care.

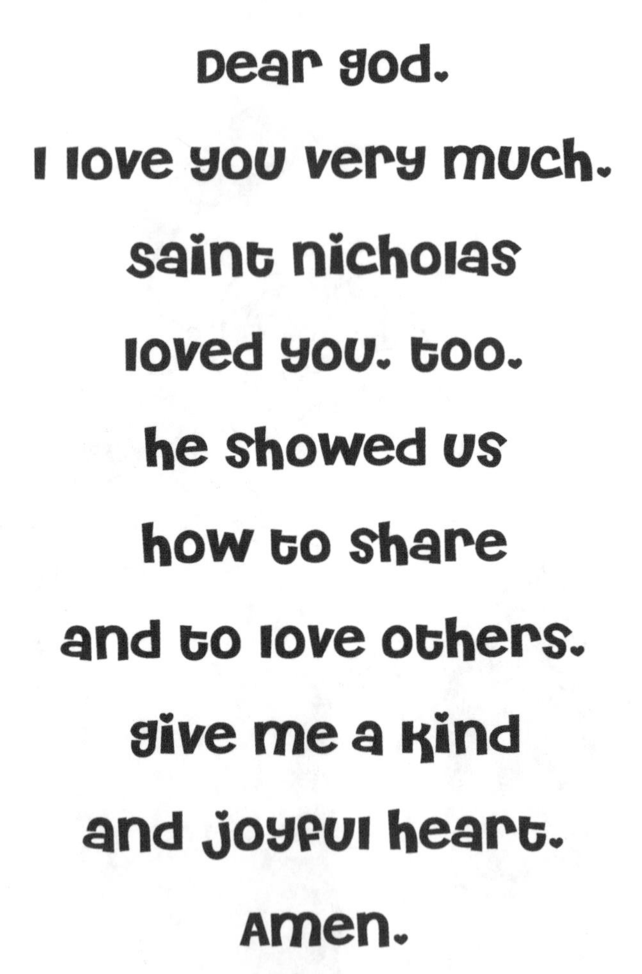

Dear God,

I love you very much.

Saint Nicholas

loved you, too.

He showed us

how to share

and to love others.

Give me a kind

and joyful heart.

Amen.

NEW WORDS (Glossary)

Bishop: A priest who is the leader of many churches in a certain area

Captain: The person in charge of a ship or boat

Defend: To stand up for or support something

Harbor: A safe area of water where boats can anchor

Innocent: Free from guilt

Inspire: To give someone an idea; to influence or encourage

Port: A place in a harbor where ships load and unload supplies

Prisoner: A person who is in prison or jail

Traditions: To pass on beliefs from parent to child

Liguori Publications
saints and me! series
SAINTS OF CHRISTMAS
Collect the entire set!
Lucy
A Light for Jesus
Francis of Assisi
Keeper of Creation
martin de porres
A Beggar for Justice
nicholas of myra
Giver of Many Gifts
Gianna Beretta molla
Wife, Mother, and Doctor
mary and Joseph
Models of Faith and Love
Saints of Christmas
Activity Book
SAINTS OF CHRISTMAS
Activity Book
Reproducible activities
for all 6 saints in the series